The Key Facts™

on

Indonesia

Essential Information on Indonesia

By Patrick W. Nee

The Internationalist®

www.internationalist.com

The Internationalist®

International Business, Investment, and Travel

Published by:

The Internationalist Publishing Company

96 Walter Street/ Suite 200

Boston, MA 02131, USA

Tel: 617-354-7722

www.internationalist.com

PN@internationalist.com

Table Of Contents

Chapter 1: Background

The Dutch began to colonize Indonesia in the early 17th century; Japan occupied the islands from 1942 to 1945. Indonesia declared its independence shortly before Japan's surrender, but it required four years of sometimes brutal fighting, intermittent negotiations, and UN mediation before the Netherlands agreed to transfer sovereignty in 1949. A period of sometimes unruly parliamentary democracy ended in 1957 when President SOEKARNO declared martial law and instituted "Guided Democracy." After an abortive coup in 1965 by alleged Communist sympathizers, SOEKARNO was removed from power. From 1966 until 1988, President SUHARTO ruled Indonesia with his "New Order" Government. After rioting toppled Suharto in 1998, free and fair legislative elections took place in 1999. Indonesia is now the world's third most populous democracy, the world's largest archipelagic state, and world's largest Muslim-majority nation. Current issues include: alleviating poverty, improving education, preventing terrorism, consolidating democracy after four decades of authoritarianism, implementing economic and financial reforms, stemming corruption, reforming the criminal justice system, holding the military and police accountable for human rights violations, addressing climate change, and controlling infectious diseases, particularly those of global and regional importance. In 2005, Indonesia reached a historic peace agreement with armed separatists in Aceh, which led to democratic elections in Aceh in December 2006. Indonesia continues to face low intensity armed resistance in Papua by the separatist Free Papua Movement.

Chapter 2: Geography

Location:

Southeastern Asia, archipelago between the Indian Ocean and the Pacific Ocean

Geographic coordinates:

5 00 S, 120 00 E

Map references:

Southeast Asia

Area:

total: 1,904,569 sq km

country comparison to the world: 15

land: 1,811,569 sq km

water: 93,000 sq km

Area - comparative:

slightly less than three times the size of Texas

Land boundaries:

total: 2,830 km

border countries: Timor-Leste 228 km, Malaysia 1,782 km, Papua New Guinea 820 km

Coastline:

54,716 km

Maritime claims:

measured from claimed archipelagic straight baselines

territorial sea: 12 nm

exclusive economic zone: 200 nm

Climate:

tropical; hot, humid; more moderate in highlands

Terrain:

mostly coastal lowlands; larger islands have interior mountains

Elevation extremes:

lowest point: Indian Ocean 0 m

highest point: Puncak Jaya 4,884 m

Natural resources:

petroleum, tin, natural gas, nickel, timber, bauxite, copper, fertile soils, coal, gold, silver

Land use:

arable land: 11.03%

permanent crops: 7.04%

other: 81.93% (2005)

Irrigated land:

67,220 sq km (2003)

Total renewable water resources:

2,838 cu km (1999)

Freshwater withdrawal (domestic/industrial/agricultural):

total: 82.78 cu km/yr (8%/1%/91%)

per capita: 372 cu m/yr (2000)

Natural hazards:

occasional floods; severe droughts; tsunamis; earthquakes; volcanoes; forest fires volcanism: Indonesia contains the most volcanoes of any country in the world - some 76 are historically active; significant volcanic activity occurs on Java, western Sumatra, the Sunda Islands, Halmahera Island, Sulawesi Island, Sangihe Island, and in the Banda Sea; Merapi (elev. 2,968 m), Indonesia's most active volcano and in eruption since 2010, has been deemed a "Decade Volcano" by the International Association of Volcanology and Chemistry of the Earth's Interior, worthy of study due to its explosive history and close proximity to human populations; other notable historically active volcanoes include Agung, Awu, Karangetang, Krakatau (Krakatoa), Makian, Raung, and Tambora

Environment - current issues:

deforestation; water pollution from industrial wastes, sewage; air pollution in urban areas; smoke and haze from forest fires

Environment - international agreements:

party to: Biodiversity, Climate Change, Climate Change-Kyoto Protocol, Desertification, Endangered Species, Hazardous Wastes, Law of the Sea, Ozone Layer Protection, Ship Pollution, Tropical Timber 83, Tropical Timber 94, Wetlands

signed, but not ratified: Marine Life Conservation

Geography - note:

archipelago of 17,508 islands (6,000 inhabited); straddles equator; strategic location astride or along major sea lanes from Indian Ocean to Pacific Ocean

Chapter 3: People and Society

Nationality:

> noun: Indonesian(s)
>
> adjective: Indonesian

Ethnic groups:

> Javanese 40.6%, Sundanese 15%, Madurese 3.3%, Minangkabau 2.7%, Betawi 2.4%, Bugis 2.4%, Banten 2%, Banjar 1.7%, other or unspecified 29.9% (2000 census)

Languages:

> Bahasa Indonesia (official, modified form of Malay), English, Dutch, local dialects (of which the most widely spoken is Javanese)

Religions:

> Muslim 86.1%, Protestant 5.7%, Roman Catholic 3%, Hindu 1.8%, other or unspecified 3.4% (2000 census)

Population:

> 251,160,124 (July 2013 est.)
>
> country comparison to the world: 4

Age structure:

> 0-14 years: 26.6% (male 34,049,541/female 32,844,509)
>
> 15-24 years: 17.1% (male 21,883,499/female 21,117,498)
>
> 25-54 years: 42.2% (male 53,766,202/female 52,325,932)
>
> 55-64 years: 7.6% (male 8,879,503/female 10,164,470)

65 years and over: 6.4% (male 7,038,904/female 9,090,066) (2012 est.)

Median age:

total: 28.5 years

male: 28 years

female: 29.1 years (2012 est.)

Population growth rate:

1.03% (2012 est.)

country comparison to the world: 112

Birth rate:

17.7 births/1,000 population (2012 est.)

country comparison to the world: 106

Death rate:

6.3 deaths/1,000 population (July 2012 est.)

country comparison to the world: 155

Net migration rate:

-1.08 migrant(s)/1,000 population (2012 est.)

country comparison to the world: 153

Urbanization:

urban population: 44% of total population (2010)

rate of urbanization: 1.7% annual rate of change (2010-15 est.)

Major cities - population:

JAKARTA (capital) 9.121 million; Surabaya 2.509 million; Bandung 2.412 million; Medan 2.131 million; Semarang 1.296 million (2009)

Sex ratio:

at birth: 1.05 male(s)/female

under 15 years: 1.04 male(s)/female

15-64 years: 1.01 male(s)/female

65 years and over: 0.78 male(s)/female

total population: 1 male(s)/female (2011 est.)

Maternal mortality rate:

220 deaths/100,000 live births (2010)

country comparison to the world: 51

Infant mortality rate:

total: 27 deaths/1,000 live births

country comparison to the world: 72

male: 31.5 deaths/1,000 live births

female: 22.2 deaths/1,000 live births (2012 est.)

Life expectancy at birth:

total population: 71.62 years

country comparison to the world: 136

male: 69.07 years

female: 74.29 years (2012 est.)

Total fertility rate:

2.2 children born/woman (2013 est.)

country comparison to the world: 104

Health expenditures:

2.6% of GDP (2010)

country comparison to the world: 184

Physicians density:

0.288 physicians/1,000 population (2007)

Hospital bed density:

0.6 beds/1,000 population (2010)

Drinking water source:

improved:

urban: 92% of population

rural: 74% of population

total: 82% of population

unimproved:

urban: 8% of population

rural: 26% of population

total: 18% of population (2010 est.)

Sanitation facility access:

improved:

urban: 73% of population

rural: 39% of population

total: 54% of population

unimproved:

urban: 27% of population

rural: 61% of population

total: 46% of population (2010 est.)

HIV/AIDS - adult prevalence rate:

0.2% (2009 est.)

country comparison to the world: 98

HIV/AIDS - people living with HIV/AIDS:

310,000 (2009 est.)

country comparison to the world: 19

HIV/AIDS - deaths:

8,300 (2009 est.)

country comparison to the world: 27

Major infectious diseases:

degree of risk: high

food or waterborne diseases: bacterial diarrhea, hepatitis A and E, and typhoid fever

vectorborne diseases: chikungunya, dengue fever, and malaria

note: highly pathogenic H5N1 avian influenza has been identified in this country; it poses a negligible risk with extremely rare cases possible among US citizens who have close contact with birds (2009)

Obesity - adult prevalence rate:

2.4% (2001)

country comparison to the world: 67

Children under the age of 5 years underweight:

19.6% (2007)

country comparison to the world: 36

Education expenditures:

3% of GDP (2010)

country comparison to the world: 141

Literacy:

definition: age 15 and over can read and write

total population: 90.4%

male: 94%

female: 86.8% (2004 est.)

School life expectancy (primary to tertiary education):

total: 13 years

male: 13 years

female: 13 years (2009)

Unemployment, youth ages 15-24:

total: 22.2%

country comparison to the world: 46

male: 21.6%

female: 23% (2009)

Chapter 4: Government and Key Leaders

Country name:

conventional long form: Republic of Indonesia

conventional short form: Indonesia

local long form: Republik Indonesia

local short form: Indonesia

former: Netherlands East Indies, Dutch East Indies

Government type:

republic

Capital:

name: Jakarta

geographic coordinates: 6 10 S, 106 49 E

time difference: UTC+7 (12 hours ahead of Washington, DC during Standard Time)

note: Indonesia is divided into three time zones

Administrative divisions:

30 provinces (provinsi-provinsi, singular - provinsi), 2 special regions* (daerah-daerah istimewa, singular - daerah istimewa), and 1 special capital city district** (daerah khusus ibukota); Aceh*, Bali, Banten, Bengkulu, Gorontalo, Jakarta Raya**, Jambi, Jawa Barat (West Java), Jawa Tengah (Central Java), Jawa Timur (East Java), Kalimantan Barat (West Kalimantan), Kalimantan Selatan (South Kalimantan), Kalimantan Tengah (Central Kalimantan), Kalimantan Timur (East Kalimantan),

Kepulauan Bangka Belitung (Bangka Belitung Islands),
Kepulauan Riau (Riau Islands), Lampung, Maluku,
Maluku Utara (North Maluku), Nusa Tenggara Barat
(West Nusa Tenggara), Nusa Tenggara Timur (East Nusa
Tenggara), Papua, Papua Barat (West Papua), Riau,
Sulawesi Barat (West Sulawesi), Sulawesi Selatan (South
Sulawesi), Sulawesi Tengah (Central Sulawesi), Sulawesi
Tenggara (Southeast Sulawesi), Sulawesi Utara (North
Sulawesi), Sumatera Barat (West Sumatra), Sumatera
Selatan (South Sumatra), Sumatera Utara (North Sumatra),
Yogyakarta*

note: following the implementation of decentralization
beginning on 1 January 2001, regencies and municipalities
have become the key administrative units responsible for
providing most government services

Independence:

17 August 1945 (declared)

National holiday:

Independence Day, 17 August (1945)

Constitution:

August 1945; abrogated by Federal Constitution of 1949
and Provisional Constitution of 1950, restored 5 July 1959;
series of amendments concluded in 2002

Legal system:

civil law system based on the Roman-Dutch model and
influenced by customary law

International law organization participation:

has not submitted an ICJ jurisdiction declaration; non-party state to the ICCt

Suffrage:

17 years of age; universal and married persons regardless of age

Executive branch:

<u>chief of state</u>: President Susilo Bambang YUDHOYONO (since 20 October 2004); Vice President BOEDIONO (since 20 October 2009); note - the president is both the chief of state and head of government

<u>head of government</u>: President Susilo Bambang YUDHOYONO (since 20 October 2004); Vice President BOEDIONO (since 20 October 2009)

<u>cabinet</u>: Cabinet appointed by the president

<u>elections</u>: president and vice president elected for five-year terms (eligible for a second term) by direct vote of the citizenry; presidential election last held on 8 July 2009 (next to be held in 2014)

<u>election results</u>: Susilo Bambang YUDHOYONO elected president; percent of vote - Susilo Bambang YUDHOYONO 60.8%, MEGAWATI Sukarnoputri 26.8%, Jusuf KALLA 12.4%

Legislative branch:

People's Consultative Assembly (Majelis Permusyawaratan Rakyat or MPR) is the upper house; it consists of members of the DPR and DPD and has role in inaugurating and impeaching the president and in amending the constitution but does not formulate national policy; House of Representatives or Dewan Perwakilan Rakyat (DPR) (560 seats, members elected to serve five-year terms), formulates and passes legislation at the national level; House of Regional Representatives (Dewan Perwakilan Daerah or DPD), constitutionally mandated role includes providing legislative input to DPR on issues affecting regions (132 members, four from each of Indonesia's origianal 30 provinces, two special regions, and one special capital city district)

elections: last held on 9 April 2009 (next to be held in 2014)

election results: percent of vote by party - PD 20.9%, GOLKAR 14.5%, PDI-P 14.0%, PKS 7.9%, PAN 6.0%, PPP 5.3%, PKB 4.9%, GERINDRA 4.5%, HANURA 3.8%, others 18.2%; seats by party - PD 148, GOLKAR 107, PDI-P 94, PKS 57, PAN 46, PPP 37, PKB 28, GERINDRA 26, HANURA 17

note: 29 other parties received less than 2.5% of the vote so did not obtain any seats; because of election rules, the number of seats won does not always follow the percentage of votes received by parties

Judicial branch:

Supreme Court or Mahkamah Agung is the final court of appeal but does not have the power of judicial review (justices are appointed by the president from a list of candidates selected by the legislature); in March 2004 the Supreme Court assumed administrative and financial responsibility for the lower court system from the Ministry of Justice and Human Rights; Constitutional Court or Mahkamah Konstitusi (invested by the president on 16 August 2003) has the power of judicial review, jurisdiction over the results of a general election, and reviews actions to dismiss a president from office; Labor Court under supervision of Supreme Court began functioning in January 2006; anti-corruption courts have jurisdiction over corruption cases brought by the independent Corruption Eradication Commission

Political parties and leaders:

Democrat Party or PD; Functional Groups Party or GOLKAR [Aburizal BAKRIE]; Great Indonesia Movement Party or GERINDRA [SUHARDI]; Indonesia Democratic Party-Struggle or PDI-P [MEGAWATI Sukarnoputri]; National Awakening Party or PKB [Muhaiman ISKANDAR]; National Mandate Party or PAN [Hatta RAJASA]; People's Conscience Party or HANURA [WIRANTO]; Prosperous Justice Party or PKS [Anis MATTA]; United Development Party or PPP [Suryadharma ALI]

Political pressure groups and leaders:

Commission for the "Disappeared" and Victims of Violence or KontraS; Indonesia Corruption Watch or ICW; Indonesian Forum for the Environment or WALHI

International organization participation:

ADB, APEC, ARF, ASEAN, BIS, CD, CICA (observer), CP, D-8, EAS, EITI (candidate country), FAO, G-11, G-15, G-20, G-77, IAEA, IBRD, ICAO, ICC (national committees), ICRM, IDA, IDB, IFAD, IFC, IFRCS, IHO, ILO, IMF, IMO, IMSO, Interpol, IOC, IOM (observer), IPU, ISO, ITSO, ITU, ITUC (NGOs), MIGA, MONUSCO, NAM, OECD (Enhanced Engagement, OIC, OPCW, PIF (partner), UN, UNAMID, UNCTAD, UNESCO, UNIDO, UNIFIL, UNISFA, UNMIL, UNMISS, UNWTO, UPU, WCO, WFTU (NGOs), WHO, WIPO, WMO, WTO

Diplomatic representation in the US:

chief of mission: Ambassador Dino Patti DJALAL

chancery: 2020 Massachusetts Avenue NW, Washington, DC 20036

telephone: [1] (202) 775-5200

FAX: [1] (202) 775-5365

consulate(s) general: Chicago, Houston, Los Angeles, New York, San Francisco

Diplomatic representation from the US:

chief of mission: Ambassador Scot A. MARCIEL

embassy: Jalan Medan Merdeka Selatan 3-5, Jakarta 10110

mailing address: Unit 8129, Box 1, FPO AP 96520

telephone: [62] (21) 3435-9000

FAX: [62] (21) 386-2259

consulate general: Surabaya

presence post: Medan

consular agent: Bali

Key Leaders:

Pres.	Susilo Bambang YUDHOYONO
Vice Pres.	BOEDIONO
Coordinating Min. for Economic Affairs	Hatta RAJASA
Coordinating Min. for the People's Welfare	Agung LAKSONO
Coordinating Min. for Political, Legal, & Security Affairs	Djoko SUYANTO
State Sec.	Sudi SILALAHI
Min. of Agriculture	SUSWONO
Min. of Communication & Information	Tifatul SEMBIRING
Min. of Defense	Purnomo YUSGIANTORO
Min. of Education & Culture	Muhammad NUH

Min. of Energy & Mineral Resources	Jero WACIK
Min. of Finance	Agus Dermawan Wintarto MARTOWARDOJO
Min. of Foreign Affairs	Raden Mohammad Marty Muliana NATALEGAWA
Min. of Forestry	Zulkifli HASAN
Min. of Health	NAFSIAH Mboi
Min. of Home Affairs	Gamawan FAUZI
Min. of Industry	Mohamad Suleman HIDAYAT
Min. of Justice & Human Rights	Amir SYAMSUDDIN
Min. of Manpower & Transmigration	Muhaimin ISKANDAR
Min. of Maritime Affairs & Fisheries	Cicip SUTARJO
Min. of Public Works	Djoko KIRMANTO
Min. of Religious Affairs	SURYADHARMA Ali
Min. of Social Affairs	Salim Segaf AL-JUFRIE
Min. of Tourism & Creative Economy	Mari Elka PANGESTU
Min. of Trade	Gita Irawan WIRJAWAN
Min. of Transportation	Evert Erenst MANGINDAAN
State Min. for Cooperatives &	Syarifuddin HASAN

Small & Medium Enterprises	
State Min. for the Development of Disadvantaged Regions	Helmy Faishal ZAINI
State Min. for the Environment	Balthazar "Berth" KAMBUAYA
State Min. for National Development Planning	Armida ALISJAHBANA
State Min. for Public Housing	Djan FARIDZ
State Min. of Research & Technology	Gusti Muhammad HATTA
State Min. for State Apparatus Reform	Azwar ABUBAKAR
State Min. for State-Owned Enterprises	Dahlan ISKAN
State Min. for Women's Empowerment & Child Protection	Linda Amalia Sari GUMELAR
State Min. for Youth & Sports	Roy SURYO
Attorney Gen.	Basrief ARIEF
Cabinet Sec.	Dipo ALAM
Dir., State Intelligence Agency (BIN)	Marciano NORMAN
Governor, Bank Indonesia	Darmin NASUTION

Ambassador to the US	Dino Patti DJALAL
Permanent Representative to the UN, New York	Desra PERCAYA

Flag description:

two equal horizontal bands of red (top) and white; the colors derive from the banner of the Majapahit Empire of the 13th-15th centuries; red symbolizes courage, white represents purity

note: similar to the flag of Monaco, which is shorter; also similar to the flag of Poland, which is white (top) and red

National symbol(s):

garuda (mythical bird)

National anthem:

name: "Indonesia Raya" (Great Indonesia)

lyrics/music: Wage Rudolf SOEPRATMAN

note: adopted 1945

Chapter 5: Economy

Economy - overview:

Indonesia, a vast polyglot nation, grew an estimated 6.1% and 6.4% in 2010 and 2011, respectively. The government made economic advances under the first administration of President YUDHOYONO (2004-09), introducing significant reforms in the financial sector, including tax and customs reforms, the use of Treasury bills, and capital market development and supervision. During the global financial crisis, Indonesia outperformed its regional neighbors and joined China and India as the only G20 members posting growth in 2009. The government has promoted fiscally conservative policies, resulting in a debt-to-GDP ratio of less than 25%, a fiscal deficit below 3%, and historically low rates of inflation. Fitch and Moody's upgraded Indonesia's credit rating to investment grade in December 2011. Indonesia still struggles with poverty and unemployment, inadequate infrastructure, corruption, a complex regulatory environment, and unequal resource distribution among regions. The government in 2013 faces the ongoing challenge of improving Indonesia's insufficient infrastructure to remove impediments to economic growth, labor unrest over wages, and reducing its fuel subsidy program in the face of high oil prices.

GDP (purchasing power parity):

$1.212 trillion (2012 est.)

country comparison to the world: 16

$1.143 trillion (2011 est.)

$1.074 trillion (2010 est.)

note: data are in 2012 US dollars

GDP (official exchange rate):

$894.9 billion (2012 est.)

GDP - real growth rate:

6% (2012 est.)

country comparison to the world: 46

6.5% (2011 est.)

6.2% (2010 est.)

GDP - per capita (PPP):

$5,000 (2012 est.)

country comparison to the world: 157

$4,700 (2011 est.)

$4,500 (2010 est.)

note: data are in 2012 US dollars

GDP - composition by sector:

agriculture: 15.4%

industry: 46.5%

services: 38.1% (2012 est.)

Labor force:

118 million (2012 est.)

country comparison to the world: 5

Labor force - by occupation:

agriculture: 38.9%

industry: 22.2%

services: 47.9% (2012 est.)

Unemployment rate:

6.1% (2012 est.)

country comparison to the world: 58

6.6% (2011 est.)

Population below poverty line:

11.7% (2012 est.)

Household income or consumption by percentage share:

lowest 10%: 3.3%

highest 10%: 29.9% (2009)

Distribution of family income - Gini index:

36.8 (2009)

country comparison to the world: 80

39.4 (2005)

Investment (gross fixed):

36.7% of GDP (2012 est.)

country comparison to the world: 9

Budget:

revenues: $164 billion

expenditures: $180.9 billion (2012 est.)

Taxes and other revenues:

18.3% of GDP (2012 est.)

country comparison to the world: 174

Budget surplus (+) or deficit (-):

-1.9% of GDP (2012 est.)

country comparison to the world: 81

Public debt:

24.8% of GDP (2012 est.)

country comparison to the world: 121

24.1% of GDP (2011 est.)

Inflation rate (consumer prices):

4.5% (2012 est.)

country comparison to the world: 123

5.4% (2011 est.)

Central bank discount rate:

6.37% (31 December 2010)

country comparison to the world: 56

6.46% (31 December 2009)

note: this figure represents the 3-month SBI rate; the Bank of Indonesia has not employed the one-month SBI since September 2010

Commercial bank prime lending rate:

11.9% (31 December 2012 est.)

country comparison to the world: 68

12.4% (31 December 2011 est.)

note: these figures represent the average annualized rate on working capital loans

Stock of narrow money:

$90.24 billion (31 December 2012 est.)

country comparison to the world: 37

$79.73 billion (31 December 2011 est.)

Stock of broad money:

$355.4 billion (31 December 2012 est.)

country comparison to the world: 29

$317.3 billion (31 December 2011 est.)

Stock of domestic credit:

$323 billion (31 December 2012 est.)

country comparison to the world: 34

$307.1 billion (31 December 2011 est.)

Market value of publicly traded shares:

$426.8 billion (31 December 2012)

country comparison to the world: 24

$390.1 billion (31 December 2011)

$360.4 billion (31 December 2010)

Agriculture - products:

rubber and similar products, palm oil, poultry, beef, forest products, shrimp, cocoa, coffee, medicinal herbs, essential oil, fish and its similar products, and spices

Industries:

petroleum and natural gas, textiles, automotive, electrical appliances, apparel, footwear, mining, cement, medical instuments adn appliances, handicrafts, chemical fertilizers, plywood, rubber, processed food, jewelry, and tourism

Industrial production growth rate:

4.1% (2011 est.)

country comparison to the world: 72

Current account balance:

-$20.73 billion (2012 est.)

country comparison to the world: 182

$2.069 billion (2011 est.)

Exports:

$188.7 billion (2012 est.)

country comparison to the world: 28

$201.5 billion (2011 est.)

Exports - commodities:

oil and gas, electrical appliances, plywood, textiles, rubber

Exports - partners:

Japan 16.6%, China 11.3%, Singapore 9.1%, US 8.1%,

South Korea 8.1%, India 6.6%, Malaysia 5.4% (2011)

Imports:

$179 billion (2012 est.)

country comparison to the world: 28

$166.1 billion (2011 est.)

Imports - commodities:

machinery and equipment, chemicals, fuels, foodstuffs

Imports - partners:

China 14.8%, Singapore 14.6%, Japan 11%, South Korea

7.3%, US 6.1%, Thailand 5.9%, Malaysia 5.9% (2011)

Reserves of foreign exchange and gold:

$103.8 billion (31 December 2012 est.)

country comparison to the world: 22

$110.1 billion (31 December 2011 est.)

Debt - external:

$187.1 billion (31 December 2012 est.)

country comparison to the world: 31

$190.7 billion (31 December 2011 est.)

Stock of direct foreign investment - at home:

$125.8 billion (31 December 2012 est.)

country comparison to the world: 32

$104.8 billion (31 December 2011 est.)

Stock of direct foreign investment - abroad:

$48.57 billion (31 December 2012 est.)

country comparison to the world: 36

$40.57 billion (31 December 2011 est.)

Exchange rates:

Indonesian rupiah (IDR) per US dollar -

9,670 (2012 est.)

8,770.43 (2011 est.)

9,090.4 (2010 est.)

10,389.9 (2009)

9,698.9 (2008)

Fiscal year:

calendar year

Chapter 6: Energy

Electricity - production:

183.4 billion kWh (2011 est.)

country comparison to the world: 24

Electricity - consumption:

158 billion kWh (2011 est.)

country comparison to the world: 24

Electricity - exports:

0 kWh (2011 est.)

country comparison to the world: 209

Electricity - imports:

2.542 billion kWh (2011 est.)

country comparison to the world: 49

Electricity - installed generating capacity:

39.9 million kW (2011 est.)

country comparison to the world: 23

Electricity - from fossil fuels:

87% of total installed capacity (2011 est.)

country comparison to the world: 83

Electricity - from nuclear fuels:

0% of total installed capacity (2011 est.)

country comparison to the world: 109

Electricity - from hydroelectric plants:

9.9% of total installed capacity (2011 est.)

country comparison to the world: 116

Electricity - from other renewable sources:

3.1% of total installed capacity (2011 est.)

country comparison to the world: 47

Crude oil - production:

912,100 bbl/day (2011 est.)

country comparison to the world: 24

Crude oil - exports:

371,400 bbl/day (2011 est.)

country comparison to the world: 22

Crude oil - imports:

265,400 bbl/day (2011 est.)

country comparison to the world: 27

Crude oil - proved reserves:

4 billion bbl (1 January 2013 est.)

country comparison to the world: 29

Refined petroleum products - production:

935,300 bbl/day (2011 est.)

country comparison to the world: 22

Refined petroleum products - consumption:

1.322 million bbl/day (2011 est.)

country comparison to the world: 19

Refined petroleum products - exports:

142,400 bbl/day (2008 est.)

country comparison to the world: 39

Refined petroleum products - imports:

407,700 bbl/day (2011 est.)

country comparison to the world: 14

Natural gas - production:

82.8 billion cu m (2010 est.)

country comparison to the world: 12

Natural gas - consumption:

41.35 billion cu m (2010 est.)

country comparison to the world: 26

Natural gas - exports:

41.25 billion cu m (2010 est.)

country comparison to the world: 10

Natural gas - imports:

0 cu m (2010 est.)

country comparison to the world: 208

Natural gas - proved reserves:

3.994 trillion cu m (1 January 2012 est.)

country comparison to the world: 12

Carbon dioxide emissions from consumption of energy:

402.1 million Mt (2011 est.)

country comparison to the world: 18

Chapter 7: Communications

Telephones - main lines in use:

> 38.618 million (2011)

> country comparison to the world: 8

Telephones - mobile cellular:

> 249.8 million (2011)

> country comparison to the world: 4

Telephone system:

> general assessment: domestic service includes an interisland microwave system, an HF radio police net, and a domestic satellite communications system; international service good

> domestic: coverage provided by existing network has been expanded by use of over 200,000 telephone kiosks many located in remote areas; mobile-cellular subscribership growing rapidly

> international: country code - 62; landing point for both the SEA-ME-WE-3 and SEA-ME-WE-4 submarine cable networks that provide links throughout Asia, the Middle East, and Europe; satellite earth stations - 2 Intelsat (1 Indian Ocean and 1 Pacific Ocean)

Broadcast media:

> mixture of about a dozen national TV networks - 2 public broadcasters, the remainder private broadcasters - each with multiple transmitters; more than 100 local TV

stations; widespread use of satellite and cable TV systems; public radio broadcaster operates 6 national networks as well as regional and local stations; overall, more than 700 radio stations with more than 650 privately-operated (2008)

Internet country code:

.id

Internet hosts:

1.344 million (2012)

country comparison to the world: 42

Internet users:

20 million (2009)

country comparison to the world: 22

Chapter 8: Transportation

Airports:

> 676 (2012)
>
> country comparison to the world: 10

Airports - with paved runways:

> total: 185
>
> over 3,047 m: 4
>
> 2,438 to 3,047 m: 22
>
> 1,524 to 2,437 m: 51
>
> 914 to 1,523 m: 71
>
> under 914 m: 37 (2012)

Airports - with unpaved runways:

> total: 491
>
> 1,524 to 2,437 m: 5
>
> 914 to 1,523 m: 24
>
> under 914 m: 462 (2012)

Heliports:

> 76 (2012)

Pipelines:

> condensate 812 km; condensate/gas 73 km; gas 7,165 km;
> oil 5,984 km; oil/gas/water 12 km; refined products 617
> km; water 44 km (2010)

Railways:

> total: 5,042 km
>
> country comparison to the world: 35

narrow gauge: 5,042 km 1.067-m gauge (565 km electrified) (2008)

Roadways:

total: 437,759 km

country comparison to the world: 14

paved: 258,744 km

unpaved: 179,015 km (2008)

Waterways:

21,579 km (2011)

country comparison to the world: 6

Merchant marine:

total: 1,340

country comparison to the world: 8

by type: bulk carrier 105, cargo 618, chemical tanker 69, container 120, liquefied gas 28, passenger 49, passenger/cargo 77, petroleum tanker 244, refrigerated cargo 6, roll on/roll off 12, specialized tanker 1, vehicle carrier 11

foreign-owned: 69 (China 1, France 1, Greece 1, Japan 8, Jordan 1, Malaysia 1, Norway 3, Singapore 46, South Korea 2, Taiwan 1, UK 2, US 2)

registered in other countries: 95 (Bahamas 2, Cambodia 2, China 2, Hong Kong 10, Liberia 4, Marshall Islands 1, Mongolia 2, Panama 10, Singapore 60, Tuvalu 1, unknown 1) (2010)

Ports and terminals:

Banjarmasin, Belawan, Kotabaru, Krueg Geukueh, Palembang, Panjang, Sungai Pakning, Tanjung Perak, Tanjung Priok

Transportation - note:

the International Maritime Bureau reports the territorial and offshore waters in the Strait of Malacca and South China Sea as high risk for piracy and armed robbery against ships; 2010 saw the highest levels of armed robbery against ships since 2007; 40 commercial vessels were attacked, boarded, or hijacked both at anchor or while underway; hijacked vessels are often disguised and cargo diverted to ports in East Asia; crews have been murdered or cast adrift

Chapter 9: Military

Military branches:

Indonesian Armed Forces (Tentara Nasional Indonesia, TNI): Army (TNI-Angkatan Darat (TNI-AD)), Navy (TNI-Angkatan Laut (TNI-AL); includes marines (Korps Marinir, KorMar), naval air arm), Air Force (TNI-Angkatan Udara (TNI-AU)), National Air Defense Command (Kommando Pertahanan Udara Nasional (Kohanudnas)) (2013)

Military service age and obligation:

18 years of age for selective compulsory and voluntary military service; 2-year conscript service obligation, with reserve obligation to age 45 (officers); Indonesian citizens only (2008)

Manpower available for military service:

males age 16-49: 65,847,171

females age 16-49: 63,228,017 (2010 est.)

Manpower fit for military service:

males age 16-49: 54,264,299

females age 16-49: 53,274,361 (2010 est.)

Manpower reaching militarily significant age annually:

male: 2,263,892

female: 2,191,267 (2010 est.)

Military expenditures:

3% of GDP (2005 est.)

Chapter 10: Transnational Issues

Disputes - international:

Indonesia has a stated foreign policy objective of establishing stable fixed land and maritime boundaries with all of its neighbors; three stretches of land borders with Timor-Leste have yet to be delimited, two of which are in the Oecussi exclave area, and no maritime or Exclusive Economic Zone (EEZ) boundaries have been established between the countries; many refugees from Timor-Leste who left in 2003 still reside in Indonesia and refuse repatriation; all borders between Indonesia and Australia have been agreed upon bilaterally, but a 1997 treaty that would settle the last of their maritime and EEZ boundary has yet to be ratified by Indonesia's legislature; Indonesian groups challenge Australia's claim to Ashmore Reef; Australia has closed parts of the Ashmore and Cartier Reserve to Indonesian traditional fishing and placed restrictions on certain catches ; land and maritime negotiations with Malaysia are ongoing, and disputed areas include the controversial Tanjung Datu and Camar Wulan border area in Borneo and the maritime boundary in the Ambalat oil block in the Celebes Sea; Indonesia and Singapore continue to work on finalizing their 1973 maritime boundary agreement by defining unresolved areas north of Indonesia's Batam Island; Indonesian secessionists, squatters, and illegal migrants create repatriation problems for Papua New Guinea; maritime delimitation talks continue with Palau; EEZ negotiations with Vietnam are ongoing, and the two countries in Fall 2011 agreed to work together to reduce illegal fishing along their maritime boundary

Refugees and internally displaced persons:

IDPs: 180,000 (government offensives against rebels in Aceh; most IDPs in Aceh, Central Kalimantan, Central Sulawesi Provinces, and Maluku) (2011)

Illicit drugs:

illicit producer of cannabis largely for domestic use; producer of methamphetamine and ecstasy

Map of Indonesia

Other Key Facts™ Titles

Key Facts on Iraq

Key Facts on Indonesia

Key Facts on South Korea

All Key Facts™ Titles are

Available at www.Amazon.com

THE INTERNATIONALIST®

2013

www.internationalist.com

www.ingramcontent.com/pod-product-compliance
Lightning Source LLC
Chambersburg PA
CBHW071649170526
45166CB00003B/1497